P9-DZZ-769

LIBRARY
FRANKLIN PIERCE COLLEGE
RINDGE NH 03461

THE
PIONEERS

KENNETH C. DAVIS
ILLUSTRATED BY RENÉE ANDRIANI

HarperCollinsPublishers

ACKNOWLEDGMENTS

An author's name goes on the cover of a book. But behind that book are a great many people who make it all happen. I would like to thank all of the wonderful people at HarperCollins who helped make this book a reality, including Susan Katz, Kate Morgan Jackson, Barbara Lalicki, Harriett Barton, Rosemary Brosnan, Dana Hayward, Maggie Herold, Fumi Kosaka, Rachel Orr, and Donna Lifshotz. I would also like to thank David Black, Joy Tutela, and Alix Reid for their friendship, assistance, and great ideas. My wife, Joann, and my children, Jenny and Colin, are always a source of inspiration, joy, and support. Without them, I could not do my work.

I especially thank April Prince for her devoted efforts and unique contributions. This book would not have been possible without her tireless work, imagination, and creativity.

We gratefully acknowledge permission to reprint the following quotations.

Page 23: Huntington Library, San Marino, California.

Page 24: Charles Fayette McGlashan Papers, BANC MSS C-B 570, Box 1, Letter to McGlashan from Georgia Ann Babcock (Donner), March 27, 1879. Courtesy of the Bancroft Library, University of California, Berkeley.

This is a Don't Know Much About® book.
Don't Know Much About® is the trademark of Kenneth C. Davis.

Don't Know Much About® the Pioneers
Copyright © 2003 by Kenneth C. Davis
Manufactured in China. All rights reserved.
www.harperchildrens.com

Library of Congress Cataloging-in-Publication Data
Davis, Kenneth C.
  Don't know much about the pioneers / Kenneth C. Davis ; illustrated by Renée Andriani.
    p.   cm.
  Summary: Explores the hardships faced by American pioneers, both on the trail and in frontier towns, using a question-and-answer format.
  ISBN 0-06-028617-2 — ISBN 0-06-028618-0 (lib. bdg.)
  1. Pioneers—West (U.S.)—History—Miscellanea—Juvenile literature. 2. Frontier and pioneer life—West (U.S.)—Miscellanea—Juvenile literature. 3. Overland journeys to the Pacific—Miscellanea—Juvenile literature. 4. West (U.S.)—History—1848–1860—Miscellanea—Juvenile literature. 5. West (U.S.)—History—1860–1890—Miscellanea—Juvenile literature. [1. Pioneers—West (U.S.)—Miscellanea. 2. Frontier and pioneer life—West (U.S.)—Miscellanea. 3. Overland journeys to the Pacific—Miscellanea. 4. West (U.S.)—History—1848–1860—Miscellanea. 5. West (U.S.)—History—1860–1890—Miscellanea. 6. Questions and answers.] I. Andriani, Renée, ill. II. Title.
F593.D27 2003
978'.02—dc21
2001024720
CIP
AC

Design by Charles Yuen
1 2 3 4 5 6 7 8 9 10
❖
First Edition

INTRODUCTION

COWBOYS AND INDIANS. QUICK-DRAW GUNSLINGERS WITH BLAZING SIX-SHOOTERS. STAGECOACHES ROLLING ACROSS THE WIDE-OPEN PLAINS. For a long time, that is how most people thought about the great American West. It is the picture that I grew up with as I watched my favorite cowboy shows on television. But that exciting Wild West show only happened in the movies.

DON'T KNOW MUCH ABOUT® THE PIONEERS tells a much more interesting story of the real people who braved harsh winters and burning summers, disease and disaster, to head west in search of a dream come true. Sometimes those dreams ended in a nightmare. And for the people who already lived in the West— the Native Americans, or Indians—the coming of the pioneers meant the end of their way of life.

Can you imagine walking thousands of miles, sometimes barefoot? Seeing grasshoppers eat an entire field of your corn? Crossing the Rocky Mountains without a map or a winter coat? Of course, you had to do it on foot, not in a comfortable air-conditioned car with a bag full of chocolate chip cookies to munch. In fact, the only chips you might get as a pioneer were "buffalo chips," which you might want to burn but certainly would not want to eat. (You can find out what buffalo chips are on page 19.) Life for boys and girls in the pioneer days was so different from our life today that it is hard to imagine how they survived. But with courage and determination, hundreds of thousands of these pioneers did.

This is their remarkable true story. I think you will find it a lot more fun and fascinating than the make-believe tales you see on television.

WHO WERE THE PIONEERS?

What is a pioneer?

A pioneer is a trailblazer—someone who leads the way for others to follow. There are pioneers of invention, like Thomas Edison. There are pioneers of ideas, like Martin Luther King, Jr., and Susan B. Anthony. But when we talk about the pioneers, we usually mean the thousands of men, women, and children who moved to the North American West between about 1840 and 1890 to build homes, farms, and eventually cities. They were families and single men and women. They were grandparents and newborns, blacks and whites, Mormons and Jews, Americans and newcomers from around the world.

With their adventurous spirits and their sharpest axes, these pioneers built much of the United States of America we know today.

Weren't there people already living in the West 150 years ago?

There sure were. Hundreds of Indian tribes had been living there for thousands of years. Europeans also lived on western lands claimed by Spain, Great Britain, and France. Yet even before the United States was born, people from the east coast of North America began pushing west. They took the *frontier,* or the boundary between settled lands and wilderness, with them.

The first frontier stood at the Appalachian Mountains. After Daniel Boone led settlers through a gap in the mountains in 1775, pioneers spread to Tennessee, Kentucky, and Ohio, then farther west to the Mississippi River. When the United States bought the Louisiana Territory from France, pioneers began looking all the way to the Pacific Ocean. Many Americans came to believe it was the fate, or *Manifest Destiny,* of the United States to stretch from sea to shining sea.

Did pioneers call themselves pioneers?

No. They called themselves "emigrants," meaning people who leave their own country for another. That's because many of the places the pioneers were going weren't part of the United States yet. When the first pioneers set out in the 1840s, the United States ended at the Missouri River. Beyond that was unorganized territory, home to Indians. And beyond that, both Great Britain and the United States claimed the Oregon Territory, which included present-day Oregon, Idaho, Washington, western Canada, and parts of Montana and Wyoming. California and the Southwest belonged to Mexico, and Texas was its very own country.

Why was President Thomas Jefferson so curious about the West?

Because Jefferson was curious about everything! Jefferson was especially curious about the West because few white people had been there when he became president in 1801. President Jefferson asked his private secretary, Captain Meriwether Lewis, to lead a group of men, or a "Corps of Discovery," across the unknown land. Lewis chose William Clark as his co-captain. In 1804, the Lewis and Clark expedition set out for the Pacific Ocean. Jefferson told the captains to make careful scientific records of the land, plants, and animals they saw and to meet peacefully with any Indians on the way. He also asked them to look for a *Northwest Passage,* or an all-water route to the Pacific.

"We were now about to penetrate a country at least two thousand miles in width, on which the foot of civilized man had never trodden; the good or evil it had in store for us was for experiment yet to determine."

—THE JOURNALS OF MERIWETHER LEWIS, APRIL 7, 1805

Lewis and Clark knew less about their destination than the first astronauts to go to the moon did—at least the astronauts had pictures!

What important shopping did Jefferson do just before Lewis and Clark set out?

He bought all of the Louisiana Territory from France in 1803. Overnight, the United States became twice as big. (The enormous territory, which stretched from the Mississippi River to the Rocky Mountains, was eventually broken into fifteen states.) The Louisiana Purchase meant that much of the land Lewis and Clark would explore now belonged to the United States.

What teenager helped make Lewis and Clark's trip a success?

A Shoshone Indian named Sacagawea. Her two-week-old son strapped to her back, Sacagawea became a guide and translator for the expedition in the spring of 1805. She gathered plants that were safe for the men to eat. She led the explorers through land she remembered from her childhood. Most importantly, she arranged for the Shoshones to sell horses to the expedition. Without these animals, the Corps of Discovery might have become stranded in the snow-covered mountains.

What did Lewis and Clark give the grizzly bear, the prairie dog, and the Great Plains?

Names! On their 8,000-mile journey to the Pacific and back, Lewis and Clark recorded and named almost 1,000 plants, animals, and landforms. One thing they didn't find was the Northwest Passage; it didn't exist.

MOUNTAIN MEN

Who blazed trails into the wilderness?

The adventurous mountain men. These rough and ready travelers were eager to trap the beavers and other animals Lewis and Clark reported in the West. Beaver fur, in particular, was worth a lot of money 200 years ago because beaver hats were fashionable in Europe. The British, French, Mexicans, and Russians had been involved in the fur trade for many years. Outdoorsmen from the United States now wanted a piece of the action.

Could mountain men be mistaken for Indians?

Some of them probably could have been. To survive in the wilderness for years at a time, the mountain men learned to live, dress, and eat like Indians. After all, Indians were the wilderness experts. Some Indians and mountain men fought, but often they met peacefully to trade. About half of the mountain men took Indian wives.

Though the mountain men learned as much as they could from the Indians, they led dangerous lives as trappers and fur traders in the wilderness. They often traveled in lands unknown to white men. Starvation, bitter storms, accidents, illness, and attacks from animals or Indians were constant threats.

Were the mountain men trappers or mappers?

All of them were trappers, and many of them went on to become mappers, too.

By the late 1830s, nearly all the beaver were gone and silk hats had become the fashion. Mountain men needed a new way to make money. Because these men knew the western wilderness so well, the United States government hired some of them to blaze and map trails for pioneers. Some early pioneers also hired mountain men to guide their journeys. Many mountain men became famous explorers. Just as Daniel Boone had done before them, trailblazers like Jedediah Smith, Jim Bridger, Joe Walker, Kit Carson, and ex-slave Jim Beckwourth found and opened important mountain passes to the West. Some of the men also became legends for their courage and daring. For instance, Jedediah Smith survived an attack by a grizzly bear. After taking nearly all of Smith's head in its mouth, the bear tore off most of Smith's ear and a large piece of skin from his head. The companion who sewed up Smith's wounds said, "This gave us a lesson on the character of the grizzly bear which we did not forget."

OREGON FEVER

How did pioneers catch Oregon Fever?

From letters, rumors, newspaper articles—anything that told of the Oregon Territory's beauty and riches. *Oregon Fever* wasn't a disease, but an overpowering desire to pick up and move to the land that is now Oregon, Washington, and Idaho. In the late 1830s, letters drifted back east from a handful of missionaries who had gone to live among the Indians. (*Missionaries* are people who want to *convert,* or change the religious beliefs of, others.) These letters convinced people that the West wasn't just a wilderness, but a land of gentle climate, fresh streams, and rich farmland. It was only a matter of time before pioneers would go to see for themselves. About one hundred set out in 1841; one thousand in 1843; and hundreds of thousands over the next fifty years.

Pioneers went west because they:

a) couldn't go east—there's an ocean in that direction.

b) heard it was paradise.

c) thought the East was getting too crowded.

d) were looking for adventure and buried treasure (gold and silver).

e) wanted free land.

f) wanted freedom.

g) all of the above.

The answer is *g*. Pioneers went west for all these reasons. Some wanted to escape the dirt, disease, and crowds of eastern cities. Others were looking for adventure or a quick fortune mining gold and silver. Still others simply wanted to live in a place where they could practice their religion freely, or—as in the case of slaves—where they themselves would be free.

Probably the most common reason for going west was the promise of free land. Many people had lost their land and savings during money troubles in 1837, and they were looking for a place to start over. The West became a land of hope, a place where people could live as they wanted, a place where they could achieve the American Dream.

Reports of the West described Oregon as a "pioneer's paradise," where "the pigs are running about under the great acorn trees, round and fat, and already cooked, with knives and forks sticking in them so that you can cut off a slice whenever you are hungry." Do you think the Oregon promoter who said this was stretching the truth?

TRUE or FALSE **Pioneers rode the 2,000 miles to Oregon in covered wagons.**

False. Most pioneers who went west did travel with wagons, but the wagons carried supplies and were packed so tightly that they had no room for passengers. Families would make wagon space for those who were sick, hurt, very young, or very old, but the most common mode of transportation for everyone else was—you guessed it—feet. Even the person driving the wagon usually walked alongside the oxen or mules that pulled the load.

How long did the journey take?

Several months. (Just think, today you can travel the same distance in a few days by car or in a few hours by airplane!) Since oxen walk only 1 to 2 miles an hour, wagon trains usually traveled 10 to 15 miles a day—fewer when they ran into storms or rough ground. If your wagon train went 10 miles a day, how many days would you spend walking the 2,000 miles to Oregon?

Answer: 200, or almost seven months

Did pioneers follow the Yellow Brick Road to Oregon?

No. Most followed the *Oregon Trail,* which certainly wasn't made of brick! In some places it was hardly a trail at all. The Oregon Trail was really many separate Indian footpaths along the Missouri, Platte,

Snake, and Columbia Rivers that mountain men had linked together. The earliest pioneers knew it as the "Emigrant Road."

Did pioneers use their best parachutes for jumping off?

No, because they weren't jumping off an airplane. They were "jumping off," as they called it, into Indian country. The main jump-off point was Independence, Missouri, at the western edge of the state. (Can you guess which state's nickname is the "Gateway to the West"?) Pioneers gathered there and in other towns along the Missouri River to make repairs, buy last-minute supplies, and get advice. They also formed wagon trains, or groups, that went west together because that was safer than traveling alone. Most trains jumped off in April or May, when there was grass for the animals to eat and time to complete the journey before winter snows fell.

"The saddest parting of all was when my mother took leave of her aged and sorrowing mother, knowing full well they would never meet again on Earth."

—MARTHA GAY, 13 YEARS OLD, WHO MOVED TO OREGON WITH HER FAMILY IN 1850

DIFFERENT DESTINATIONS

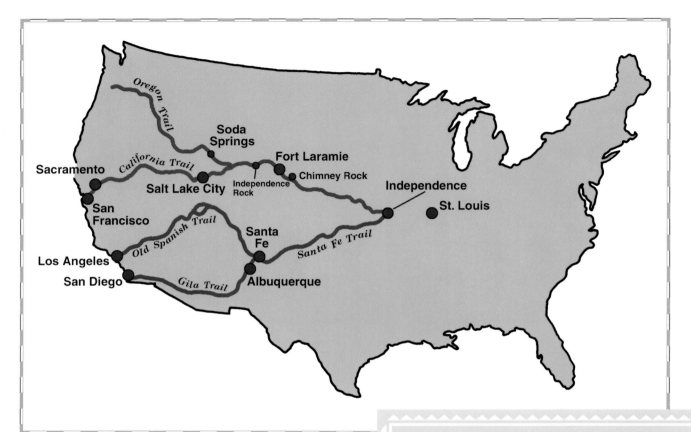

Was the Oregon Trail the only route west?

No, it was just the best known and most traveled. Several other trails left Missouri for different places in the West. These routes included the Gila and Old Spanish Trails, which led to San Diego and Los Angeles, and the Santa Fe Trail, a trading route to New Mexico. Settlers also went to Texas on various smaller trails that began in Missouri and Mexico.

California, Texas, and the Southwest were once part of Mexico. When Mexico became free of Spain in 1821, it welcomed thousands of Americans into Texas. Soon there were more English-speaking Americans and their slaves in Texas than Mexicans! These newcomers wanted to set up an independent, English-speaking Republic of Texas. Mexican leader Antonio López de Santa Anna didn't like that at all. In 1836, he defeated Davy Crockett and others at the famous battle of the Alamo. Soon other Americans defeated him, and Texas became a separate country (until it became a state nine years later).

Were there Pilgrims on the trail?

No, not the Pilgrims who sailed on the *Mayflower*—but other *pilgrims* did travel west.

BRIGHAM YOUNG

A pilgrim is someone who makes a pilgrimage, or a journey to a holy land. Among the pioneers were members of a religious group called the Mormons, or the Church of Jesus Christ of Latter-day Saints. The Mormons had moved from New York to Ohio to Missouri to Illinois. They were chased from state to state because many Americans disagreed with their beliefs. In 1846, their leader, Brigham Young, took a small group of Mormons to find a place where they could practice their religion freely. When the group came to the dry land near the Great Salt Lake in present-day Utah, Young said, "This is the place." Thousands of additional Mormons followed. Working together, they made the desert bloom.

So what was inside all those wagons?

Everything that would fit. Anything you needed on the trip,
or would need when you arrived, you had to take with you.
There weren't any real stores out west. There were a few forts,
but if they had any extra supplies when you got there, they'd
be wildly expensive.

Can you guess how the pioneers
kept their eggs and fragile dishes
safe in the bumpy wagons? They
packed them in their barrels of
flour and cornmeal!

Pioneers packed their wagons with hundreds of pounds of
food—per person! For each traveler, guides recommended
bringing at least 200 pounds of flour, 75 pounds of bacon, 30
pounds of hardtack (hard bread), 25 pounds of sugar, 10
pounds of rice, 10 pounds of salt, 5 pounds of coffee, 2 pounds
of tea, and various amounts of dried beans and fruit, baking
soda, and cornmeal. Along with all that, families crammed the

wagons with pots and pans, dishes, extra clothing, tools and spare wagon parts, medicine, sewing supplies, and cash (for toll bridges, ferries, and the purchase of replacement wagon parts or food along the way). Pioneers also managed to squeeze in pieces of furniture, cookstoves, books, and a few keepsakes. All this in a space only about as big as a minivan!

Why were wagons called "prairie schooners"?

Because they had tall white canvas tops that looked like ships' sails. When wagons traveled across the Great Plains (the wide open *prairies,* or grasslands, of the American Midwest), tall prairie grasses hid the wagons' wheels from view and made the wagons look, from a distance, like a fleet of ships in an ocean of grass. So wagons were nicknamed "prairie schooners" or "ships of the plains."

The best prairie schooners were strong, yet lightweight. To help make them waterproof, pioneers covered the wooden bottom with tar and the white canvas top with oil. The top, which was stretched over five or six U-shaped bows, could be closed in the back using a drawstring if the weather was bad. Hooks on the inside and outside of the wagon held milk cans, tools, and women's bonnets. Spare wagon parts were stored underneath the flooring.

Many families turned their canvas wagon covers into moving billboards that announced their names or destinations, or carried determined slogans like "Patience and Perseverance" or "Oregon or the Grave."

A Day on the Trail

What served as an alarm clock on the trail?

Rifles shot into the air—at 4 A.M.! If you were a pioneer, your day started before sunrise. Before the wagons were on their way at 7 A.M., there was much to do. In the darkness, the women and older girls began building fires. They cooked breakfast, took care of the babies and young children, cleaned up, pulled down tents, and packed the wagons. At the same time, men and boys rounded up the cattle, yoked the oxen, and went hunting. Younger children helped gather fuel for the fire, feed the animals, and milk the cows. How would you like to do all those chores—before school?

Have you ever had a breakfast of "slamjohns and sowbelly"?

If you've had pancakes and bacon, you have. The pioneers liked to start the day with a hearty breakfast. They usually had some combination of bacon and cornmeal cakes, pancakes, or hardtack; sometimes with beans, fried meat, and gravy. Everyone, including children, drank coffee because plain water often tasted so bad that even animals would not drink it. Some families drove their cattle along with them, so they had fresh milk to drink.

Lunch meant cold leftovers, and the evening meal brought more of the same if the men had bad luck hunting. Fresh meat, fish, and wild berries were favorite trail meals.

TRUE or FALSE Buffalo chips were a trail treat.

Pioneers liked these chips, but not as snacks! *Buffalo chips* were dried buffalo droppings. Because they burned well, the chips were handy for lighting cooking fires on the treeless plains. Children found other uses for the chips as well, such as throwing them at one another or seeing who could make them sail the farthest. How would you like to toss that kind of Frisbee?

When the wagon train stopped for the night, the wagons parked in a big, closed circle. This created a kind of fort, with the pioneers and their livestock staying inside for protection from wild animals and Indians. Men took turns keeping watch through the night.

19

TRAIL CHORES

How often did pioneers change their clothes on the trail?

About as often as they bathed—not very often at all! Most pioneers wore the same dirt-encrusted clothes day after day. It wasn't easy to find clean water for washing, which pioneer women probably thought was just as well. Laundry was an awful chore that took an entire day.

To keep their dresses from dragging in the mud, women wore their skirts a little higher than they had back home. A few daring women wore the new fashion of *bloomers,* or loose pants that were gathered at the ankles. Men and boys wore linen or woolen pants and shirts. To protect their faces and eyes from the sun, men and boys wore wide-brimmed hats and women and girls wore bonnets. Everyone wore sturdy shoes or boots.

How did pioneer children learn their lessons on the trail?

Since there was no school to attend, some parents gave their children lessons on the trail. Other children just read the few books they brought along, kept journals, and wrote letters to friends and family.

But even more than spelling and math, children's biggest lessons were probably the ones taught by trail life itself. Pioneer children learned how to identify new plants and animals, how to fix things when they broke, and how to invent and adjust to new ways of doing things (like using buffalo chips for firewood!).

Parents learned things along the trail, too. Pioneer women discovered that the bumpy wagons churned their butter for them if they just left the milk can hanging on its hook!

How did the pioneers learn what was up ahead?

From those who'd gone before them. By 1845, many pioneers owned guidebooks, like *The Emigrants' Guide to Oregon and California,* written by scouts and earlier travelers. The books described landmarks along the trail and gave advice on where best to cross rivers and camp for the night.

Sometimes pioneers learned what was up ahead from *go-backs,* discouraged pioneers who had turned around to go back east. These travelers were said to have "seen the elephant." This expression suggested they'd seen something new and different—the hardships of the West—and didn't want any part of it.

To see for themselves what was coming up, some members of the wagon train rode ahead on horses. An even better source of information, pioneers found, was a message system called the "roadside telegraph": notes from earlier travelers scrawled on paper and attached to trees, placed under rocks, or wedged into notched sticks stuck into the ground. Other times pioneers painted their messages right onto rocks or onto the skulls of cows, oxen, deer, or even humans. Some messages were notes to friends, but others warned of danger. One message read, "Look at this—look at this! The water here is poison, and we have lost six of our cattle. Do not let your cattle drink on this bottom."

TRAIL DANGERS

What was the greatest danger to pioneers on the westward trails?

a) accidents   c) Indians

b) sickness   d) buffalo

All these things were dangerous, but the answer is *b*. Of the thousands of pioneers who died on the journey west, most were victims of diseases such as cholera, measles, smallpox, typhoid, or dysentery. Pioneers did have medicines and herbs, but no one knew much about treating these diseases.

> "One day a [buffalo] herd came in our direction like a great black cloud, a threatening moving mountain, advancing toward us very swiftly and with wild snorts, noses almost to the ground and tails flying in midair. . . . One [wagon] was completely demolished and two were overturned. Several persons were hurt."
>
> —FROM THE DIARY OF CATHERINE HAUN, A YOUNG BRIDE, **1849**

Accidents were the next biggest cause of death. Children fell from the wagon and were crushed under its wheels; people were trampled in buffalo stampedes or drowned during river crossings; men on watch at night shot one another by accident. Travelers got lost, starved, froze to death, or unknowingly drank alkali water, which contained deadly mineral salts. Very few were killed by Indians. (In fact, pioneers killed more Indians than the other way around.)

No one knows how many pioneers traveled west on the overland trails, but the number is probably somewhere between 250,000 and 650,000. We do know that at least 20,000 people died on the journey, which averages about ten graves per mile of trail.

How did the pioneers and Indians get along?

Sometimes they fought, but most meetings were peaceful enough. Indians often came up to wagon trains, hoping to trade buffalo meat or horses for guns, tobacco, cloth, food, or metal fishing hooks. Some Indians even acted as scouts or helped ferry pioneers across rivers. Indians who looked warlike were usually headed to fight an enemy tribe, though some young tricksters did like to steal pioneers' animals. Still, pioneers were afraid of the Indians. In 1847, the United States government set up forts along the trails to help protect the pioneers.

Pioneer and Indian children were fascinated by one another. Ten-year-old Kate McDaniel wrote about the daughter of a Sioux Indian chief who visited her camp in 1853:

"She was about fifteen years old and . . . very beautiful. . . . The little princess, as we liked to call her, let us pet her pony and then she showed us how she could ride and what her pony could do. . . . Then [she] jumped into her saddle, waved her hand to us, and with a little giggling laugh, was gone like a beautiful bird."

If you were a pioneer's stove, where might you end up?

In a furniture graveyard along the trail! As wagons headed into the mountains, many families had to lighten their loads for the tired oxen. Heavy stoves and furniture were often left behind, no matter how treasured they were. Pioneers abandoned dressers, tables, chairs, food, books, stoves, fine china, trunks, tools, bedding, and even a piano.

OTHER WAYS WEST

When is a shortcut not a shortcut?

"It rained and snowed so hard that the few animals we had were covered by the snow. . . . Families shared with one other as long as they had anything to share, making each one's portions very small. The hides were boiled, and the bones were burned brown and eaten. We tried to eat a decayed buffalo robe, but it was too tough and no nourishment in it; some of the few mice that came in camp were caught and eaten."

—SURVIVOR GEORGIA DONNER, WHO WAS FOUR YEARS OLD WHEN SHE CROSSED THE MOUNTAINS

When it makes your trip longer instead of shorter. This was the kind of shortcut taken by the Donner Party, a wagon train of eighty-nine people led by George Donner in 1846. Their guidebook recommended a shortcut through the mountains, but the book's author had never actually taken the route himself. The bad advice led to one of the worst disasters of the westward movement. The Donner Party was stranded in the Sierra Nevada mountains for the winter, where nearly half its members starved to death. Those who lived did so by eating animal hides, twigs, and even their shoes. Finally, as people died, the survivors ate the bodies of their dead companions to stay alive.

Could you get to the West faster by hiring a coach?

Yes, if you mean a stagecoach, not a football coach. Beginning in 1858, stagecoaches could take you west from Missouri in just twenty-five days. Stagecoaches, large closed carriages pulled by horses, bumped and jumbled along all day and all night. They stopped for less than an hour each day for passengers to eat. About every 12 miles, they changed horses. Riding in a stagecoach was like sitting in a stiff, cramped armchair for three weeks without changing your clothes.

TRUE or FALSE Pioneers could travel west by boat.

True. You know that Lewis and Clark's expedition found no all-water route to the West. However, pioneers could travel from the east coast to the west coast by sailing all the way around South America. (That was a journey of 13,000 miles!) Pioneers could also sail to Panama, walk or ride horses across the 50-mile strip of land, and hope to catch a ship sailing back up the west coast of North America. These routes were more expensive—but rarely more comfortable—than the overland route. The sea journey took from six months to a year, during which nearly all the passengers got seasick and bored on board.

What was the best part of the trail?

Reaching the end of it! Actually, the dangers and difficulties of the trail were only the beginning of the hardships the pioneers would face. By the time they arrived in Oregon or California, pioneers were exhausted. Most were nearly, if not completely, out of supplies. But there was no time to waste. Winter was coming quickly, and they needed a place to live.

Many pioneers built temporary houses called "lean-tos"—simple log shelters left open on one side—to live in while they began working on a cabin. Others lived in their wagons while they worked. (Oh, how tired they were of those wagons!) Then they took their wagons apart and used the wood to build furniture or pieces of their new home.

How long did it take to raise a log cabin?

a) three weeks   c) one day

b) two months   d) one year

Believe it or not, the answer is *c*. It took a long time to clear the land and prepare logs for a cabin. Still, if a family did that ahead of time and the neighbors came to help, they needed only one day to raise a one-room log cabin. (Pioneer families could raise log cabins all by themselves; it just took longer.)

Why were pioneer families so big?

Because more children meant more pairs of hands to help do the work. In pioneer days, people worked from sunup to sundown. They had to make everything from soap to bread to candles to clothes by hand.

Even the youngest children had chores to do. They gathered eggs, nuts, berries, and fuel for fires. They weeded the gardens, fed the chickens, and watched the fields to drive away squirrels and birds who ate the corn. Older children helped make jams, jellies, butter, candles, soap, and medicines. They fetched water, milked cows, plowed, planted, washed, ironed, mended, and looked after the younger children. No wonder one pioneer woman wrote, "A lazy person should never think of going to Oregon."

Believe it or not, most girls on the frontier were married before they were sixteen. Soon after that, they were starting families of their own.

Was there time for school on the frontier?

A little. In the early days of the frontier, children were taught at home because people lived so far away from one another. Even when more settlers arrived, some children did not go to school because their parents needed their help at home. Those who did go usually attended one-room schoolhouses where children of all ages were taught together. Often the teacher wasn't much older than some of his or her students!

Some teachers had a hard time making teenage boys behave. Young men who had driven teams of oxen across the continent and maybe even fought Indians or shot grizzlies didn't want to be told what to do! One California teacher made it clear he was the boss by placing a six-shooter on his desk on the first day of school and saying, "We're here to learn. If anyone misbehaves, there's going to be trouble."

It wasn't all work on the frontier. Children did find time to climb trees, jump rope, visit swimming holes, and play tag, hopscotch, and hide-and-seek. They also played with homemade marbles, checkers, tops, and rag or cornhusk dolls.

Would you get mail on the frontier?

Yes, but at first you'd have to wait a long time for letters because mail service wasn't very regular. When stagecoaches began running in 1858, mail service got much better.

Even speedier than the stagecoaches was the Pony Express. This famous mail service from St. Joseph, Missouri, to Sacramento, California, whisked letters across nearly 2,000 miles in just ten days. Brave young horseback riders rode at top speed all day and all night, even in snow and sleet or through the desert. Each rider rode 70 miles and changed horses six times before he handed the mail off to the next man. The Express was in business about nineteen months before telegraph lines connecting the East and West made it unnecessary in 1861.

SETTLING THE PLAINS

Why did the first pioneers pass up all the land on the Great Plains?

Because they thought the wide-open spaces between the Mississippi River and the Rocky Mountains were much too . . . plain. Early explorers had looked over the flat, windy, treeless land and named it "The Great American Desert." For many years pioneers believed the plains could not be farmed and were a place fit only for Indians.

What changed pioneers' minds about the plains?

Wie geht's?

As areas farther west filled up, many people were still hungry for land. To open up room on the plains, the United States government began pushing Indians who lived there onto *reservations,* or small pieces of land that were set aside for them. In 1862, the government passed the

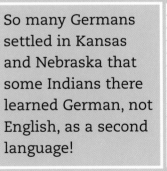

So many Germans settled in Kansas and Nebraska that some Indians there learned German, not English, as a second language!

Homestead Act. This act gave 160 acres of land (about nine football fields' worth) to anyone who paid a $10 filing fee and agreed to work and improve the land for five years. Within months, thousands of settlers had moved to Kansas and Nebraska. They found out that the land they now owned was no desert, but it was dry and challenging to farm.

How do you build a house where there isn't any wood?

The same way you light a fire without it—you use what's there. Pioneers who settled on the Great Plains became known as "sodbusters" because they cut up the *sod* (grass with the roots and dirt still attached) to clear fields and build their houses. These sturdy "soddies" were cool in the summer and warm in the winter, and they wouldn't go up in flames in a prairie fire. Even so, the houses leaked when it rained and were impossible to keep clean. Worse, snakes and mice were known to work their way through the sod walls and ceiling and occasionally "drop in" for dinner!

One homesteader, a doctor named Brewster Higley, was so fond of his new Kansas home that he wrote a poem about it in 1872. The following year, a neighbor set the poem to music, and soon everyone was singing "Home on the Range":

Oh, give me a home where the buffalo roam,

Where the deer and the antelope play,

Where seldom is heard a discouraging word,

And the skies are not cloudy all day.

Which were the hardest things about living on the Great Plains?

a) flooding and tornadoes

b) drought, dust storms, and prairie fires

c) blizzards and frigid winters

d) grasshoppers devouring crops

e) loneliness

Take your pick—all these dangers were part of living on the plains. Tornadoes and floods in the spring gave way to hailstorms and drought in the summer. Hot, dry weather stirred up dust storms and made conditions perfect for prairie fires. Some years grasshoppers flew in and ate nearly everything in sight, ruining crops in a matter of hours. The insects would eat leather, cloth, curtains, fence posts, door frames, and food in cupboards. When winter came, bitter cold and blizzards killed people caught outside.

But for some, the worst thing was the year-round loneliness. Neighbors could be a mile or two away, but sometimes as distant as thirty miles. The whole world seemed to be only grass and sky and sky and grass.

One woman of the plains became famous for her series of Little House books, which describe her life on the prairie. You might've read these books. Do you know who the woman is?

ANSWER: LAURA INGALLS WILDER

THE GREAT CALIFORNIA GOLD RUSH

Who were the forty-niners before they were San Francisco's football team?

They were the thousands and thousands of gold seekers who rushed to California in 1849 (get it?—forty-niners?) in hopes of getting rich. In 1848, a carpenter named James Marshall had found gold in a stream near Sutter's Mill, California. Word of his discovery spread like wildfire. Gold hunters streamed in from across America and around the world.

Was mining for gold exciting?

No. It was awfully hard work, and people rarely struck it rich. Miners spent long days squatting at the edge of a stream, shoveling and picking at rock, shaking their heavy pans to clear the gold specks from the dirt. They worked in wind and rain and sometimes even stood waist deep in freezing water.

Most miners were young, single men. They lived in rough-and-tumble camps and towns that had equally rough-and-tumble names: Poverty Hill, You Bet, Squabbletown, Git Up and Git, Mad Ox Ravine, Chucklehead Diggings, and Humbug Canyon were just some of the most descriptive.

There were so few women in California during the gold rush that one miner walked 16 miles just to see a lady!

Who called California "Gold Mountain"?

The Chinese. Many Chinese sailed across the Pacific Ocean when they heard about the gold rush because there were wars going on in China and lots of people there were out of work. But life in California wasn't much better for the Chinese. When frustrated white gold hunters didn't get rich, they wanted to take out their anger on someone. They picked the Chinese. Soon Chinese immigrants were forced into jobs like washing clothes or rolling cigars. They had to live apart from everyone else, they had no rights, and they had to pay extra taxes. Many eventually went home. Those who stayed often started Chinatowns in the cities where they settled.

TRUE or FALSE Mining for gold was the best way to get rich during the gold rush.

False! Most of the people who got rich from the gold rush made their money from the miners, not from the gold. How? All those thousands of miners needed food, clothing, and supplies. Prices went sky-high: Flour was $800 a barrel; shovels were $100 apiece. The miners especially needed sturdy pants to wear while they bent, dug, and squatted. The pants that were invented to meet their need might be the same kind you're wearing right now—jeans, made by Levi Strauss.

TRUE or FALSE **Indians traveled from east to west before the pioneers did.**

True. Unfortunately, they moved for an entirely different reason—they were forced.

From the time Columbus landed in North America, Indians' lives would never be the same. At first, Indians and Europeans often met as friends and traders. But the friendships didn't last. The newcomers wanted land, and the land belonged to the Indians. As the settlers pushed farther into Indian lands, they fought the Indians, took their land without asking, and signed *treaties* (agreements between nations) forcing or tricking them into giving it up.

In 1830, President Andrew Jackson signed the Indian Removal Act. This act meant that Indians in the East were forced to leave their homelands and go to the Indian Territory west of the Mississippi River.

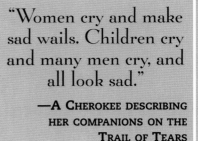

> "Women cry and make sad wails. Children cry and many men cry, and all look sad."
>
> —A CHEROKEE DESCRIBING HER COMPANIONS ON THE TRAIL OF TEARS

What was the Trail of Tears?

The *Trail of Tears,* or the "Trail Where They Cried," as the Cherokees called it, was a terrible forced march from the tribe's sacred homelands in Georgia, North Carolina, and Tennessee to the Indian Territory in the West. In the late 1830s, soldiers forced young and old at bayonet point through blinding blizzards and freezing temperatures. Four thousand Cherokees, or one in every four, died of cold and starvation on the journey. More died of disease and poor living conditions once they reached the hot, dry land that is now Oklahoma.

What did the Plains Indians think about the first pioneers?

At first, the coming of white settlers seemed to many Indians to be a good thing. A number of Indian tribes, including the Dakota, Comanche, and Cheyenne, lived on the Great Plains in the 1800s. The tribes that were part of the fur trade especially liked getting guns and other goods that made them more powerful than their enemies.

But soon the Indians realized that the white people brought bad things, too. The worst, more deadly than any weapon, was disease. European germs such as smallpox, measles, and influenza wiped out huge numbers of Indians across North America.

Which pioneers lived in their saddles?

Cowboys. Not all pioneers came west to claim land and settle down. Some came to ride the wide-open spaces, rope cattle, and make their livings as cowboys. Most cowboys were young, poor, and had little education. They came from many places—the South, the East, the Midwest, and even as far away as Europe. About one in six was Mexican, and about the same number were black. Some were full- or half-blood Indians. Some weren't cowboys at all—they were cowgirls.

TRUE or FALSE **Cowboys spent their days taming a mess of bucking broncos.**

False. Cowboys' days were dirty, dangerous, and often dull. Their job was to poke, prod, and guide longhorn cattle north from Texas to railway towns on the plains. For each day cowboys were on a cattle drive (which took two to three months), they spent at least fourteen hours on horseback. Cowboys rode through quicksand, among rattlesnakes, insects, and hostile Indian tribes, and in sun, rain, wind, sleet, hail, and even snow. Their days were so long and their pay so low that only one out of three cowboys returned for more than one drive.

One of the most famous cowboys was a former slave named Nat Love. In a rodeo in 1876, Nat won so many roping and shooting contests that he was nicknamed "Deadwood Dick." Another former slave, Bill Pickett, became a famous rodeo star for inventing *bulldogging,* or wrestling a steer to the ground by pulling on its horns. Sometimes he would drag it down while biting its lower lip!

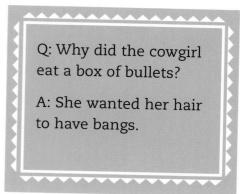

Q: Why did the cowgirl eat a box of bullets?

A: She wanted her hair to have bangs.

How much water did a cowboy's ten-gallon hat hold?

bandanna

lariat

saddle

chaps

boots

spurs

Not ten gallons! In fact, the word *gallon* probably came from the Spanish word *galón,* referring to the braid around the hat. But a sturdy, wide-brimmed hat *could* hold enough water to refresh a cowboy's horse. It also served as an eye shade when he took a nap, a fan when he was hot, and a mini-umbrella that protected him from sun and rain.

A cowboy also wouldn't be much of a wrangler without his trusty:

- chaps, worn over his pants to protect his legs

- bandanna, to keep the dust out of his nose and mouth

- boots, to keep his feet in the saddle and protect him from thorns and snakes

- spurs, to urge his horse on

- lariat, or rope, to catch stray cattle; and— most of all—

- his saddle, which was his driver's seat, his office, and often his pillow at night

What was the "Iron Horse"?

a) a child's toy

c) the fastest horse in the West

b) a bucking bronco

d) the railroad

The answer is *d.* The "Iron Horse" is what the Indians called the trains that began crossing the West in the 1860s. Railroads had been used in the East since the 1820s, but in 1863 construction began on a *transcontinental,* or coast-to-coast, railroad.

Building a railroad across North America was no easy task. All the materials had to be brought in from the East. Workers had to line up every 500-pound rail by hand and hammer each spike into place. They had to blast tunnels through the mountains and build bridges over rivers and valleys. It was backbreaking work.

Thousands and thousands of men built the transcontinental railroad. Many were soldiers who had fought in the Civil War. Many others were immigrants, especially from China and Ireland. The Chinese were often given the most dangerous jobs, such as lighting explosives. Though the Chinese became experts at their jobs, thousands died to build the railroad.

Why were workers racing to finish the railroad?

Because two companies were competing to lay down the track. The Central Pacific started from California and built east, while the Union Pacific started from Nebraska (where the eastern railroad lines left off) and built west. The companies raced because whoever laid more track got more money and more land from the government. In the end, the Central Pacific laid 690 miles of track, while the Union Pacific laid 1,086.

Where could you find the most famous rail nail in the West?

At Promontory Summit, Utah. At that spot in 1869, railroad officials hammered in the golden spike that joined the east and west tracks of the transcontinental railroad. (They pulled the spike out and replaced it with an ordinary iron one when the ceremony was over.) The railroad turned the five-month wagon journey into a trip of just eight days. At first, the train was a dirty and uncomfortable way to travel. Most passengers sat in straight-backed wooden seats and put up with the steam and ashes that blew in through the open windows. Still, it was the fastest way west, and those who could afford it used it. The railroad brought thousands of new pioneers to the plains. It also tied America together in a whole new way. People, news, goods, and crops could travel between the East and the West as never before.

"Buffalo Bill" got his nickname from all the buffalo he killed to feed the railroad workers. The Plains Indians, who depended on the buffalo to support themselves, were forced onto reservations as the animals disappeared. That's just what the American government wanted. Can you guess why? Pioneers wanted the Indians' land.

Did buildings in frontier towns wear disguises?

Yes. The prairie towns that sprang up along the railroad had sod buildings, just like prairie farms. To make the towns look nicer than they really were, owners covered shops and businesses on the main street with two-story wooden masks, or *false fronts*. Each frontier town had at least a post office, hotel, saloon, general store, stable, blacksmith shop, and newspaper. These shops lined one main street that started at the railway station. Raised sidewalks on each side of the street kept people out of the dirty, muddy roadway—unless, of course, they had business on the other side!

Where in the West will you find haunted houses?

In ghost towns! Actually, ghost towns are towns that no one lives in anymore. Many mining towns in the West became ghost towns because everyone picked up and left when the gold or silver was gone. Railroad towns, on the other hand, were the most likely to survive because it was easy for people and goods to come and go.

The residents of Merna, Kansas, were so upset that the railroad passed them by, they took their whole town apart and rebuilt it next to the tracks!

How wild was the Wild West?

The West was wild, especially compared to the more civilized East. But it wasn't as wild as it's often made out to be in movies and television. For many years, the West didn't have many sheriffs, jails, or courts of law, because the settlements were too new and the distances between them too great. To keep outlaws from running wild, pioneers took matters into their own hands by forming *vigilante* groups. These were usually groups of property owners who wanted to protect their belongings. Vigilantes could keep crime under control, but by taking the law into their own hands they sometimes punished innocent people.

Even when real lawmen like Wyatt Earp, Doc Holliday, and Wild Bill Hickok did arrive on the frontier, western towns were generally less mannerly than their eastern counterparts. A sign at a dance in Kansas commanded PLEASE DON'T SPIT ON THE FLOOR!

What famous outlaw was really just a kid?

Billy the Kid (whose real name was Henry McCarty) was only seventeen years old when he killed his first man. The Kid was caught many times and put in jail. He usually escaped because his big wrists and small hands helped him get out of handcuffs easily. Though legend says Billy the Kid killed twenty-one people, he probably really killed four or so before a sheriff shot him at age twenty-one.

INDIAN WARS

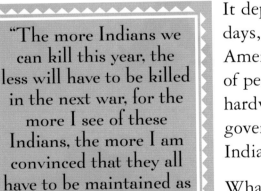

Were the pioneers heroes?

> "The more Indians we can kill this year, the less will have to be killed in the next war, for the more I see of these Indians, the more I am convinced that they all have to be maintained as a species of paupers."
>
> —GENERAL WILLIAM T. SHERMAN, 1867

It depends on whom you ask. To most people in pioneer days, and to many people today, the settling of the American West was a heroic achievement. The thousands of people who started new lives in the West were brave, hardworking, and resourceful. But the United States government gave them land that really belonged to the Indians.

What the pioneers gained, the Indians lost. Indians had to give up their sacred lands and their way of life as they were pushed onto small reservations in the worst areas of the plains. They weren't allowed to hunt, dance, practice their religion, or do their traditional crafts. The United States was supposed to supply food, but there was never enough. Life on the reservations was terrible.

Did the pioneers and Indians ever go to war?

Yes. Whites and Indians had been fighting off and on ever since settlers arrived in the New World. But between 1865 and 1890, as pioneers flooded into the West, so many battles flared up that they are now called the Plains Indian Wars. Army officers stationed at forts in the West were called upon both to fight and to make treaties with the Indians. Of the 400 treaties the United States made with the Indians, our government broke every single one.

"We preferred our own way of living. We were no expense to the government. All we wanted was peace and to be left alone. Soldiers were sent out in the winter, who destroyed our villages. Then Long Hair [Custer] came in the same way. They say we massacred him, but he would have done the same thing to us had we not defended ourselves and fought to the last."

—SIOUX LEADER CRAZY HORSE, JUST BEFORE HE DIED IN 1877

The Indians had a special name for the black soldiers they fought—"buffalo soldiers." The soldiers' black curly hair reminded the Indians of the hair of the buffalo. Since the Indians thought the buffalo sacred, the soldiers proudly took on the name. Buffalo soldiers served in nearly 200 battles and won seventeen Medals of Honor for bravery.

Who made sure the Battle of the Little Bighorn was Custer's Last Stand?

CRAZY HORSE

Sioux and Cheyenne warriors, led by Sitting Bull and Crazy Horse. These Indians defeated Lieutenant Colonel George A. Custer at the Little Bighorn River in 1876. Since not a single man in Custer's force was left standing, and Custer himself was killed, the battle is also called "Custer's Last Stand." Little Bighorn was the Indians' biggest—and last— victory.

GEORGE A. CUSTER

What was the Indians' "last stand"?

The Battle of Wounded Knee in 1890. The fight began while Dakota Indians were giving up their weapons to the United States Army at Wounded Knee, South Dakota. One of the Indians fired a shot—maybe by accident— and the army shot back. The soldiers killed about 200 unarmed Indians, including Sioux Chief Big Foot. The Indian Wars were over.

SITTING BULL

THE END OF THE FRONTIER

What happened to the frontier?

It disappeared. By 1890, so many pioneers had come west that most open lands had been settled.

The last area to be settled was the Oklahoma Territory. The Oklahoma Land Rush was a sight to see! At high noon on April 22, 1889, thousands of people lined up on the border of the territory. At the sound of a pistol, they charged on horseback, wagon, and on foot to claim land. (Those who "jumped the gun" and took off the night before the rush were called "Sooners." That's where Oklahoma gets its nickname, the Sooner State.) Twelve hours later, what had been just an expanse of prairie became Guthrie, a city of 10,000 people complete with 500 houses and thousands of tents.

What did the pioneers leave us?

They left us wagon-wheel ruts on the Oregon Trail, for one thing! (Yes, you can still see them in some places.) More importantly, the pioneers left us with a sense of who we are as Americans. Many people say that the "pioneering spirit"—of curiosity, hard work, determination, resourcefulness, individualism, and love of freedom—is what America is all about.

Oregon Trail
Crossed Here

Time Line

1400	More than 300 Indian tribes exist in North America.
1492	Christopher Columbus reaches North America.
1540	Spanish explorer Francisco Vásquez de Coronado travels north from New Spain (Mexico) into what is now Kansas; claims New Mexico for Spain.
1600	French *coureurs de bois* ("forest runners") begin working with Indians to trap North American beavers.
1607	Jamestown, the first permanent English settlement in America, is founded.
1620	The Pilgrims land at Plymouth, Massachusetts.
1670	Britain's Hudson's Bay Company controls the fur trade in northern North America.
1682	René La Salle claims the Mississippi Valley for France.
1763	England gains land between the Appalachian Mountains and the Mississippi River from France at the end of the Seven Years' War.
1775	Daniel Boone opens the Wilderness Road through the Cumberland Gap of the Appalachian Mountains.
1776	The American colonies declare independence from Great Britain.
1803	President Thomas Jefferson buys the Louisiana Territory.
1804	Lewis and Clark set out to explore the land between Missouri and the Pacific Ocean.
1811	First practical steamboat ride to the West.
1821	Mexico gains independence from Spain and begins trading with the United States; the Santa Fe Trail opens.
1830	The U.S. Congress passes the Indian Removal Act.
	The Church of Jesus Christ of Latter-day Saints is founded in New York State.
1831	Cyrus McCormick invents the mechanical reaper, which harvests 100 acres in the time it had taken to harvest 8.
	The Cherokees fight removal to Oklahoma in court but are forced to move anyway; the Trail of Tears begins.
1836	Texas wins independence from Mexico and becomes its own republic.
	Missionaries travel west on the Oregon Trail.
1837	John Deere invents the steel plow, which cuts through thick prairie soil easily.
	Financial panic and depression hit the United States.
1838	The Cherokee Indians are forced west on the Trail of Tears.
1841	The first wagon trains set out on the Oregon Trail.

1845	Texas becomes part of the United States.
1846	The Latter-day Saints leave Illinois and head west, settling at the Great Salt Lake in 1847.
1848	The Oregon Territory becomes part of the United States.
	Gold is discovered in California.
1858	The first overland stagecoaches reach California.
1860	The Pony Express begins.
1861	The U.S. Civil War begins.
	The Pony Express operation ends as telegraph lines extend across the country.
1862	The Homestead Act grants 160 acres of public land to anyone willing to live on and improve that land for five years.
1865	The U.S. Civil War ends.
1866	Jesse Chisholm organizes the first great cattle drive from Texas to Abilene, Kansas.
1869	The Golden Spike is driven at Promontory Summit, Utah, connecting the two ends of the transcontinental railroad.
	Women in Wyoming become the first in the United States to be granted the right to vote.
	Major John Wesley Powell explores the Colorado River and Grand Canyon.
1872	Yellowstone becomes the first national park.
	The Montgomery Ward catalog makes ready-made goods available on the frontier.
1873	Joseph Glidden invents barbed wire, eliminating the free ranges of the West.
1876	Sioux and Cheyenne warriors defeat General Custer at the Battle of the Little Bighorn.
	Grasshoppers are declared "Public Enemy #1" in Minnesota, and the government offers children up to fifty cents for every bushel of dead grasshoppers collected.
1877	Chief Joseph and the Nez Perce Indians, just 30 miles from freedom in Canada, surrender to the U.S. Army.
1883	William "Buffalo Bill" Cody organizes the first Wild West Show.
1886	Apache warrior Geronimo surrenders to U.S. troops.
1890	The U.S. Army defeats the Sioux Indians at Wounded Knee.
	The U.S. government declares the American frontier officially closed.

ADDITIONAL RESOURCES

To learn more about the pioneers and westward expansion, you can visit these and other historic sites and museums:

- Donner Memorial State Park and Emigrant Trail Museum, Truckee, California

- Sutter's Fort State Historic Park, Sacramento, California

- Western Historic Trails Center, Council Bluffs, Iowa

- Jefferson National Expansion Memorial/Museum of Westward Expansion (Gateway Arch), St. Louis, Missouri

- National Frontier Trails Center, Independence, Missouri

- Chimney Rock National Historic Site, Bayard, Nebraska

- Oregon Trail Museum/Scotts Bluff National Monument, Gering, Nebraska

- End of the Oregon Trail Interpretive Center, Oregon City, Oregon

- National Historic Oregon Trail Interpretive Center, Baker City, Oregon

- Fort Laramie National Historic Site, Fort Laramie, Wyoming

- Independence Rock, 48 miles south of Casper, Wyoming

Or, check out these pioneer-related websites:

- End of the Oregon Trail
  www.endoftheoregontrail.org

- Trail of Tears
  www.rosecity.net/tears

- Jefferson National Expansion Memorial/Museum of Westward Expansion
  www.nps.gov/jeff/main.htm

- Oregon-California Trails Association
  www.octa-trails.org

Franklin Pierce College Library

00145271

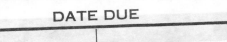
DATE DUE